SIZZLING *Celebrities*

Josh!

LEADING MAN JOSH HUTCHERSON

BY
SHERRI MABRY
GORDON

Enslow Publishers, Inc.
40 Industrial Road
Box 398
Berkeley Heights, NJ 07922
USA
http://www.enslow.com

Library of Congress Cataloging-in-Publication Data:

Gordon, Sherri Mabry.

  Josh! : leading man Josh Hutcherson / Sherri Mabry Gordon.
     pages cm. — (Sizzling celebrities)
  Includes index.
  Summary: "Read about Josh's early life, how he got started in acting, and his future plans"—Provided by publisher.
  ISBN 978-0-7660-4200-1
  1. Hutcherson, Josh—Juvenile literature. 2. Actors—United States—Biography—Juvenile literature. I. Title.
  PN2287.H877G67 2014
  791.4302'8092—dc23
  [B]
                          2012040316

Future editions:
Paperback ISBN: 978-1-4644-0343-9
EPUB ISBN: 978-1-4645-1012-0
Single-User PDF ISBN: 978-1-4646-1012-7
Multi-User PDF ISBN: 978-0-7660-5822-4

Printed in the United States of America

052013 Lake Book Manufacturing, Inc., Melrose Park, IL

10 9 8 7 6 5 4 3 2 1

To Our Readers: We have done our best to make sure all Internet addresses in this book were active and appropriate when we went to press. However, the author and the publisher have no control over and assume no liability for the material available on those Internet sites or on other Web sites they may link to. Any comments or suggestions can be sent by e-mail to comments@enslow.com or to the address on the back cover.

♻ Enslow Publishers, Inc., is committed to printing our books on recycled paper. The paper in every book contains 10% to 30% post-consumer waste (PCW). The cover board on the outside of each book contains 100% PCW. Our goal is to do our part to help young people and the environment too!

Photo Credits: AP Photo/Amy Sancetta, p. 8; AP Photo/Arthur Mola, p. 36; AP Photo/Charles Sykes, pp. 24, 38; AP Photo/Eduardo Perdugo, p. 31; AP Photo/Evan Agostini, pp. 16, 20; AP Photo/Jennifer Graylock, p. 13; AP Photo/Joel Ryan, p. 23; AP Photo/Katy Winn, pp. 6, 27; AP Photo/Kirkland, p. 12; AP Photo/Matt Sayles, pp. 4, 44; AP Photo/Rob Griffith, p. 1; Shea Walsh/AP Images for Nintendo, p. 19; AP Photo/Stephen Chernin, p. 11; AP Photo/Tammie Arroyo, pp. 9, 15; AP Photo/Thomas Padilla, p. 28; AP Photo/Vince Bucci, p. 40.

Cover Photo: AP Photo/Rob Griffith (Josh Hutcherson at the premiere of *Journey 2: The Mysterious Island* in 2012.)

Contents

It didn't take long for Josh Hutcherson to become a big star.

Meet Josh!

Although Kentucky-born Josh Hutcherson had been acting since he was nine, it was his role as Peeta Mellark in *The Hunger Games* that made him a star. He quickly became a bona fide heartthrob. With more than a million likes on Facebook and just as many followers on Twitter, *The Hunger Games'* star has catapulted into the spotlight.

In fact, Josh says it's still mind-blowing when he thinks about the success and popularity of *The Hunger Games*. "I think we all kind of knew there was a pretty big fan base for the books, but I never expected people to be this crazy about it and it to be this successful," Josh told Reuters.

Yet, the popularity and success hasn't affected who Josh is. In fact, when it comes to young teen actors, none are as down-to-earth and charming as Josh.

Kentucky Boy

Born in Union, Kentucky, on October 12, 1992, Joshua Ryan Hutcherson is truly Kentucky blue. After all, his parents, Chris and Michelle Hutcherson, were also born and raised in Kentucky.

With Christmas lights up year-round, a couch on his front porch, and his face painted blue for Kentucky Wildcats basketball games, Josh is proud of his southern heritage. It has made him the person he is today.

"I'm the same person in public that I am back home, so I don't put on an act or anything like that," says Josh.

The Making of a Star

Anyone who followed Josh's performance in *The Hunger Games* can tell he has a real passion for acting. But acting is not a new talent that he picked when he landed the role of Peeta. Acting is who Josh is at the core. From the time he was little, he knew he wanted to be an actor.

In fact, he has always liked entertaining people. He also admits he was pretty good at it, playing hooky from school by acting like he was sick.

"I'm the kid who was always putting on a show," Josh told the *Post-Bulletin*.

◀ *Josh Hutcherson hugs an excited fan during* The Hunger Games *mall tour in March 2012.*

No one in his family is in the entertainment business. So when four-year-old Josh began telling his parents he wanted to be an actor, they didn't take him seriously. But Josh was relentless.

By the time he was nine years old, Josh was getting antsy about starting his career. When begging and pleading with his parents failed, he took matters into his own hands. He got out the phone book and dialed a Cincinnati talent agency. Finally, his parents paid attention and started to consider giving him the shot he was begging for.

By January 2002, at the suggestion of a talent agent, Josh and his mom left Kentucky and went to Los Angeles to audition for television pilots. Pilots are sample episodes of television programs being considered by television networks.

"My parents saw my passion and saw that I wasn't going to stop at least until I went [to Los Angeles] and had a go at it," Josh told *Dolly* magazine. "So they supported me."

A Family Guy

Leaving Kentucky for L.A. was not an easy decision though. Josh has a close-knit family and is especially close to his younger brother, Connor. Additionally, Josh and his mother did not want to leave behind family and friends permanently. Instead, they commuted to Los Angeles from Kentucky.

They stayed in a small studio apartment in L.A. while Josh was working and auditioning and would return home to Kentucky for a few days when he wasn't busy. It was the only option they could think of. His parents didn't want to uproot the whole family for something that came with no guarantees.

A Diamond in the Rough

When it comes to acting, Josh has what experts call raw talent and natural abilities. Although he has never had an official acting lesson, he instinctively knows how to perform. Once in L.A., nine-year-old Josh showed that he had what it takes to build a career. First, he won a role in the pilot *House Blend*, a WB comedy. Then came an Animal Planet movie, *Miracle Dogs.* He also did some guest shots on *ER*, Lifetime's *The Division,* and *Line of Fire*.

Then, within a year, Josh appeared in the film *American Splendor*, which won the grand jury prize at the Sundance Film Festival. He also landed small parts in *Eddie's Father* and *Motocross Kids*.

◄ *Josh Hutcherson (center) and the actors who play his parents, Ted Shackelford and Kate Jackson, hold their scripts during a break from filming* Miracle Dogs.

Building Bridges

By 2004, Josh's expressive voice helped him land some voice talent roles in major motion pictures. He got the chance to work alongside some top talent. In fact, it wasn't long until he was working with Tom Hanks on *The Polar Express*, a computer-animated feature. He did the voice for the boy hero.

Josh also did the voice for Markl, the wizard Howl's assistant in *Howl's Moving Castle*. He was the voice of Toad in *Party Wagon* and the voice of Van-El in the *Justice League* television episode, "For the Man Who Has Everything ."

Tom Hanks stands next to ▶ a poster for the film The Polar Express, *which also features Josh Hutcherson.*

Even though there is no live action in voice parts, Josh says the work is still tiring. For example, he did all the voice parts of Markl in one day. By the end of the day, he could barely talk.

When It Rains, It Pours

By the time Josh was thirteen, the roles seemed to pour in. After voicing characters, Josh started landing more live-action roles. For instance, in 2005, Josh impressed audiences as the young hero in the movie *Little Manhattan*. Critics said he showed maturity beyond his years for his ability to play a young boy who struggles with his parents' separation.

In 2006, Josh played Walter in *Zathura: A Space Adventure*, which is a story about a board game that shoots its players into an outer-space adventure. His character is forced to protect his younger brother and his older sister, played by Kristen Stewart (*Twilight*). Josh won a Young Artist Award for the film.

Taking the Next Step

When Josh landed a supporting role in the comedy *RV*, he got the opportunity to work alongside Robin Williams, and he loved every minute of it. Josh can see now why so many people think Robin Williams is incredibly funny.

"I don't know how we got any work done. We were constantly laughing," Josh told the *Cincinnati Post* "...I tried to stay to [the script]. But it was hard to keep up with him. Sometimes the script would just say 'Robin patter' [which means Robin was supposed to just say whatever came to his mind. So] he would just ramble on."

In the movie, Williams plays an overworked, frazzled father who tricks his family into going on an RV trip to Colorado. Meanwhile, Josh plays the son of Williams's character, who is a weightlifting, hip-hop-loving kid.

▲ Robin Williams (center) sits with screaming fans on MTV's Total Request Live. Williams starred with Josh Hutcherson in the film RV.

▲ Josh Hutcherson and his costar AnnaSophia Robb attend the premiere of Bridge to Terabithia on February 3, 2007.

Although *RV* did not make a lot of money compared to other movies, it was still important to Josh's career. The movie helped him go from a child actor to a teenage actor. What's more, it gave Josh exposure to a more adult audience. Josh followed up his role in *RV* with a role as a troubled teen in *Firehouse Dog*.

Crossing the Bridge

Then, in 2007 Josh nabbed a starring role in *Bridge to Terabithia*, a movie adapted from Katherine Paterson's much-loved book. In the movie, Josh was able to show Hollywood that

Josh Hutcherson signs ▶ *posters for his movie* Firehouse Dog *on April 1, 2007.*

not only can he handle action, he also can handle emotional scenes really well.

In *Bridge to Terabithia*, Josh plays an aspiring artist and outcast who discovers an imaginary world with another outcast student. Josh received lots of praise for his work in this film and he won two awards. He won two Best Young Artist awards—one for Best Leading Actor and one for Best Ensemble.

In 2008, Josh did a darker movie called *Fragments*. This movie is a drama about the survivors of a mass murder spree. In it, Josh plays a young man who is struck mute after witnessing the murder of several restaurant patrons by a crazed gunman.

Since going to Los Angeles as a nine-year-old, Josh consistently landed acting jobs. He hit his teen years with an impressive resume.

The Journey Begins

Josh is always up for an adventure—especially when it involves acting. And his roles seem to show that. For example, the characters he has played have traveled into space in *Zathura* and across the country in *RV*. So when a role in *Journey to the Center of the Earth* opened up, it seemed like a natural fit.

In 2008, Josh landed the role of Sean Anderson in the first *Journey* movie, which helped cement his career as a crush-worthy teen star. Josh was fifteen at the time of the movie. But he played a thirteen-year-old who travels to Iceland with a scientist-uncle he barely knows, played by Brendan Fraser. The movie was one of the first live-action features shot entirely in 3D.

"It [was] the future of filmmaking," Josh told *Speedway* magazine. "I definitely [wanted] to be part of the cutting edge... [with] the whole new technology in 3D, you experience the movie—you're not just watching it. You're the fourth person along for the adventure."

Journey to the Center of the Earth is based on an 1860s novel by Jules Verne. In the movie, Fraser's character has some ideas that have made people think he is crazy. But on a trip to Iceland, he and his nephew, played by Josh, make a major

discovery. And they
are launched into a
thrilling journey deep
beneath the earth's
surface. They travel
through never-before-
seen worlds and
encounter a variety of
creatures.

Because the movie
was filmed in Hawaii,
Josh stayed in a house
on the beach. He liked
coming home from work and swimming in the ocean. He also
got up early and would go surfing in the morning before work.

Filming the movie required a lot of physical activity, and Josh
loved every minute of it. "[That's] actually one of the reasons
why I signed up to do the movie because I love stunts and I love
sports…" Josh told *Knox News*.

One of his favorite parts to film was the scene where he
crosses a bottomless gorge by jumping from one floating
magnetic rock to another. When filming the scene, there was a

green screen behind him and he had to jump on different rocks, each with a different mechanism. One rock was on air pistons, one rock was on an inner tube, and one flipped him all the way around.

▲ Josh Hutcherson (right) and Brendan Fraser joke around on MTV's Total Request Live. They appeared on the show to promote their movie Journey to the Center of the Earth.

"I love getting to do any kind of [physical] activity," Josh said on JHutcherson.net. "So getting to do these stunts was awesome for me. I had a field day with it."

While filming *Journey to the Center of the Earth*, Josh spent much of the time covered in mud, which was fun in the beginning. But after awhile, he said it got a little old.

"After about day 30 of being in mud, it's like 'I'm sort of over it,'" he told About.com. "But we've been to all these beautiful places and it's usually really nice out."

Freaked Out

In 2009, Josh played Steve in *Cirque du Freak: The Vampire's Assistant*, which is a movie based on the books by Darren Shan. In the movie, Josh's character is a vampaneze, which is a really vicious vampire. "[Vampaneze] do whatever they want, whenever they want," Josh told About.com. "They're just the rulers of the world."

Steve is unlike any other character Josh had played before, because he is such a bad guy. In fact, Josh says Steve starts off on the wrong path and just continues down that road in the movie. Yet, despite Steve's bad reputation, Josh really wanted the role of Steve because he's so different and so unlike him that he thought it would be really fun.

"It was cool to play a bad guy," Josh told *TeenHollywood*. "...I read [the script] early on before it got settled as to who was going to play what role...but for me, I was more interested in [playing] Steve because it was something I'd never really taken on before. I loved getting to play the bad guy and kind of unleash the evilness."

Josh had a blast shooting the movie in a creepy graveyard and old movie theater in New Orleans. While filming the movie, he and co-star Chris Massoglia, who plays Darren, played basketball together.

Although Josh admits that he didn't read the book, he says he kind of wanted it that way. He felt if he read the books that he would know too much about the character and wouldn't be able to make it his own.

"I liked not knowing and just going into it with a fresh mind," Josh told *TeenHollywood*. "My younger brother has read all the books and my grandma has, which is kind of weird."

He's All Right

In another big career move, Josh landed the role of Laser in the movie *The Kids Are All Right*. The movie is about the teen son and daughter of two moms who want to find their biological father. Once they find him, they introduce him to their moms. But when they do, it creates a number of problems for the family, especially when one of the mothers takes a romantic interest in him.

Josh enjoyed the role of Laser because it felt so real. "As a teenager, [Laser] was going through a point in his life where he's trying to figure out who he is and how he fits into his

Josh takes a break during the 2010 Sundance Film Festival to play the Wii video-game system. He was at the festival to promote The Kids Are All Right.

world and who are his friends and exactly what his relationship is with his family," Josh told About.com.

As for getting into character, Josh believes Laser really wanted a relationship with his father and that's why he encouraged his sister to help with the search.

"I don't think [Laser] necessarily needs to have the father figure, but I think he just wants a guy that he can hang out with that's somewhat of a fatherly figure," Josh told About.com. "I think that a lot of people in life...don't have fathers and they have the yearning to know what that's like."

The Kids Are All Right begins and ends with shots of Josh as Laser, which is a nice perk for Josh. But he had no idea that's what the director had in mind.

"I didn't realize it was going to begin and end on me, which is kind of cool. I think the ending was really nice because it was sort of that hope... [It gives] you a good feeling of hope at the end where you knew that maybe not everything was okay right now, and this family's definitely going to have some more problems down the road, but they're going to be all right."

In 2010, the movie was nominated for an Oscar for Best Picture. So Josh made good on his promise to his mother and took her as his date to the Oscars. This gesture showed fans everywhere that he really is just as down to earth and likable as he claims to be. Although the movie didn't win any awards, Josh and his mom had a great time.

He was excited that the movie gained so much attention, and he felt it was well deserved. To him, the movie was important because the storyline was authentic. It also showed family life in a way that had never been done before.

As for the movie's impact on his career, *The Kids Are All Right* was a step in the right direction for Josh as well. It helped him become more of an adult actor because he got to portray real life instead of a fantastical world.

"I've done a lot of the fantastical crazy stuff that doesn't exist," Josh explained. "So to break it down into something that was so real and genuine like this was really fun and different."

4 Hungry for More

After Josh's success in *Journey to the Center of the Earth* and *The Kids Are All Right*, it was clear he was hungry for more challenging roles—parts he could really connect with. So when he read the part of Peeta in *The Hunger Games*, Josh knew instantly that the role was for him.

Josh said he identified with Peeta from the start because he maintains his integrity even in times of war. He also connected with Peeta's ability to communicate with people and his ability to turn on the charm when he needs to.

"Peeta, for me, has a really strong belief that you can't just become a piece in someone else's game," Josh told About.com. "You've got to be the controller of your own life and who you are as a person and I believe in that 100 percent."

Additionally, the action-packed *Hunger Games* was right up Josh's alley as well. When he was growing up, Josh spent a lot of time outdoors both playing sports and exploring the countryside around him. Some of his favorite pastimes included rock climbing, mountain biking, and camping. So the idea of playing a young man who navigates treacherous terrain was appealing.

In fact, Josh admits he has never wanted a role as badly as he wanted the role of Peeta. In his heart, he knew he was perfect for the part. But he wasn't sure if the director felt the same way.

"The two weeks of waiting to find out if I got the job [was hard]," Josh told *Total Film* magazine.

Josh admits he wasn't sure what he would do if he didn't get the part. He wanted it that badly. But he had nothing to worry about. Once director Gary Ross and *The Hunger Games* author Suzanne Collins saw him, they knew he was the Peeta they had been searching for.

In fact, author Suzanne Collins was present for Josh's audition. When he performed the scenes in which Katniss fights to keep Peeta alive in the cave, she said she became a true believer in Josh's ability to play Peeta.

Josh Hutcherson appears ▶ *at the British premiere of his biggest movie yet,* The Hunger Games.

▲ *After they had acted in* The Hunger Games, *Josh Hutcherson and Jennifer Lawrence signed copies of the book on which the film was based.*

"People may get thrown, say, by the color of an actor's hair, or something physical," Collins said. "But I tell you, if Josh had been bright purple and had six-foot wings and gave that audition, I'd have been like 'Cast him! We can work around the wings.' He was that good."

Total Transformation

The Hunger Games takes place in the ruins of what was once North America. Every year, the Capitol of the nation of

Panem forces each of its twelve districts to send a teenage boy and a teenage girl to compete in the Hunger Games. In the movie, Josh's character, Peeta Mellark, along with Jennifer Lawrence's character, Katniss Everdeen, represent District 12.

To prepare for the role of Peeta, Josh had to really bulk up. He needed to gain a lot of muscle and strength. In four weeks, he put on fifteen pounds of pure muscle by training with a former Navy SEAL.

Josh worked out five days a week pulling weighted car tires across a gym floor with a rope. He also hit a punching bag with a baseball bat until his arms were numb. And he ate about 4,000 calories a day. His diet consisted mainly of chicken, eggs, spinach, and broccoli.

In the meantime, Josh needed to undergo another transformation as well. His dark brown hair had to become blonde for him to look like Peeta. And this was not an easy task. It took several attempts by the stylists before they got it right.

"It was a little terrifying because at first they tried to do it without bleaching, but it turned orange and then this weird green," Josh told *People* magazine. "Finally they bleached it out and it worked."

But by the end of the four weeks, he looked like Peeta. And he had the stamina needed to act in *The Hunger Games*, which involved running through the woods, dodging arrows and firebombs, and escaping from monsterlike creatures.

Putting It All Together

Filming of *The Hunger Games* took place in North Carolina. The film crew used an abandoned village to represent District 12 and the forests to represent the inside of the arena.

As for the filming, Josh says his favorite scene in the movie is the cave scene because it's where Peeta declares his love for Katniss. And he admits that kissing his co-star Jennifer Lawrence, who played Katniss, was pretty good too.

"Of course I liked kissing her," Josh told *US* magazine. "I mean come on! She's beautiful."

Yet, despite the connection Katniss and Peeta share on the screen, it wasn't quite enough for them to win the coveted Best Kiss Award from MTV. Instead, that honor went to Robert Pattinson and Kristen Stewart in *The Twilight Saga: Breaking Dawn Part 1*. But Josh was excited for the pair, who were also dating at the time.

"Honestly, you know what? I've never really felt it to be a competition. And I wish I could pretend it was 'cause it'd be fun," Josh said after the awards. "Their cast is fantastic, our cast is fantastic and there's never been any bloodshed...not yet."

Just for Fun

When they weren't busy filming, the cast and crew enjoyed some of the local establishments. One of their favorites was Early Girl Eatery, which according to Josh has the best

▲ Josh Hutcherson and Jennifer Lawrence spent a lot of time together while filming and promoting The Hunger Games.

breakfasts. He also enjoyed a local movie theater that served full meals during the movies.

The actors also enjoyed playing basketball together—and playing pranks on one another. And Josh appears to be skilled at both.

Hunger Games co-star Jack Quaid openly admits that "Josh is an insane basketball player" and that Josh wiped the floor with him. While Jack Quaid was in awe of Josh's basketball-playing abilities, Jennifer Lawrence, who played Katniss, is less than enthusiastic about his prankster skills.

"I pranked Jennifer [Lawrence] once," Josh admits. "I put a life-sized dummy in her trailer bathroom that had a mangled face. She went to go to the bathroom and opened the door and there was the dummy and she apparently peed her pants."

All in all, *The Hunger Games* was a highly successful movie, bringing in a whopping $152.5 million on its opening weekend at the box office. By the end of its run in movie theaters, it had taken in $685 million worldwide. As a result, Josh became an instant star.

The Journey Continues

But *The Hunger Games* wasn't the only movie Josh did that year. In fact, he has had a steady stream of work, which is more than some of the big-name actors can say.

◀ The cast of The Hunger Games got really close on the set. Here, from left, actors Liam Hemsworth, Jennifer Lawrence, Josh Hutcherson, and Elizabeth Banks join director Gary Ross for a photo at the French premiere of the film.

Earlier in 2012, Josh starred in *Journey 2: The Mysterious Island*. This movie was a sequel to *Journey to the Center of the Earth*. But with the exception of Josh, not many of the original cast returned. He said when he saw the new list of cast members he was pleasantly surprised because he would never have expected all of them to ever be in the same movie.

Journey 2 centers on Josh's character, Sean Anderson, who receives a coded message from his grandfather. After deciphering the message, Sean and his stepfather, played by Dwayne Johnson, set out to the mysterious island.

Their characters meet up with a tour guide and his strong-willed daughter, played by Vanessa Hudgens. Together, they set out to find the island. Once there, they realize they only have a short amount of time to get off the island. They need to escape its powerful seismic waves before it gets buried underwater completely.

The film features several near-death experiences, including one in which Josh's character must fight for his life despite having an injured leg. Because it's a water scene, Josh was required to become a certified scuba diver.

Additionally, Josh physically feels like he is up for almost anything. So in the movie, he did some of his own stunts. For instance, in some of the scenes, they had him hooked to a rig and hoisted him 25 feet in the air. "I'm a producer's worst nightmare because I'm always trying to do my own stunts,"

Josh said to *Total Film Magazine.* "[In one scene] I was flying on top of a giant bumblebee and I fell off and rolled my ankle severely. It was pretty gnarly."

Because there was a gap of a few years in between the two *Journey* movies, Josh says it actually felt like a completely new movie. The movie was shot in the secluded areas of Oahu in Hawaii, which has a lot of foliage and wildlife.

"I'd look down, and there would be an ant, and then I'd look closer and see there were, like, nine million anthills around us," Josh told a Canadian news source. "It dawned on me, 'I'm not in Kentucky anymore.' I'm in a jungle."

Dwayne Johnson, a former wrestler known as The Rock, was impressed with Josh. And he enjoyed partnering with him in the action sequences.

"I also appreciate that he's coming into his own, and becoming a man at the same time," Johnson told a Canadian news source. "He has great poise."

A Very Busy Year

Despite doing two big movies in 2012, Josh didn't stop there. He also was in *Red Dawn, 7 Days in Havana,* and *The Forger* (originally titled *Carmel*).

Red Dawn is a remake of a 1980s movie. It's about the Communists invading the United States and a group of teens who try to save the country.

Although the remake of *Red Dawn* was actually filmed a few years earlier, its release was delayed to November 2012 due to MGM's financial difficulties. Still, Josh was excited about this movie because he has always wanted to be in a "shoot 'em up" movie. Plus, the storyline is one that he finds fun and exciting.

"I'm a fan of war and action movies," Josh said on jhutcherson. net. "I've always wanted to do one, and *Red Dawn* is a classic so many people love. It's a really cool story about kids fighting for something much bigger than them....It was an awesome shoot too. I got to fire so many different types of weapons and blow up so much stuff. I loved it."

Meanwhile, *7 Days in Havana* is a collective film in which each director shoots one episode that takes place from morning to

In Journey 2: ▶ The Mysterious Island, *Josh Hutcherson got to act with Vanessa Hudgens and Dwayne "The Rock" Johnson.*

night. In the movie, people in Havana keep bumping into one another and lead double lives.

Josh plays a tourist in the segment titled "Monday." The segment is done documentary style and follows him around as he explores the culture of the island for the first time.

In *The Forger*, Josh plays a troubled fifteen-year-old who is abandoned and finds himself in Carmel, California. In the movie, he is a talented artist who is introduced to the world of art forgery. While there, he makes friends with a retired artist played by Lauren Bacall.

Hollywood Takes Notice

Not only did Josh stay busy throughout 2012, but he also had a very successful year. For instance, he won the Next Mega Star award at the fifth annual NewNowNext Awards, which honors actors who are on the verge of pop culture explosion.

Josh also won the Breakthrough Performer of the Year Award from CinemaCon. CinemaCon is the official convention of The National Association of Theatre Owners (NATO), which is the largest and most important gathering of cinema owners and operators around the world.

"With an already impressive resume of films under his belt, [Josh] is one of the most accomplished young actors of his time," said Mitch Neuhauser, managing director of CinemaCon. "With the release of *The Hunger Games*, [Josh] is poised to take the movie world by storm, and we could not be more excited to present such a talented young actor, with [this award]."

Josh also won the Best Male Performance at the MTV Movie Awards in 2012 for his role as Peeta. And the odds were in favor of *The Hunger Games*, which also took home the most golden popcorn-shaped trophies of the evening. In addition to Josh's award, the movie also won Best Fight for the film's final three-way battle and the Best On-Screen Transformation for Elizabeth Banks's over-the-top portrayal of Effie Trinket. And Jennifer Lawrence won the Best Female Performance for her role as Katniss Everdeen.

"I've wanted to hold a Golden Popcorn since I was like four years old," Josh told the crowd when he accepted the award. "This is incredible. It's insane too, because every single one of those actors [up for this award], I admire…so to even be up here is blowing my mind right now."

Winning the award puts Josh on a long list of A-list actors who have previously won the award, including Arnold Schwarzenegger, Denzel Washington, Brad Pitt, Tom Cruise, and Leonardo DiCaprio.

After winning the award, Josh referred to himself as "the little guy from Kentucky that could." He also gave a shout-out to his fans: "You guys are the best fans in the world. You're crazy and passionate and you make our job amazing."

But winning the award wasn't the only highlight of the evening for Josh. He also got to see his *Zathura* co-star, Kristen Stewart.

"I actually got to talk to Kristen Stewart tonight for the first time in five years," Josh told *MTV News*. "That was awesome to connect with her again, especially after everything that's happened to the both of us [with *Twilight* and *The Hunger Games*]."

Josh has fond memories of filming *Zathura* with Kristen. They had a lot of fun together, and he learned a lot working with her. She even gave him a pet turtle for his birthday.

What's Next?

With *The Hunger Games* under his belt, Josh is excited to get to work on the second movie in Suzanne Collins's trilogy, *Catching Fire*. This time around, he will be working with a new director, Francis Lawrence. Although Josh really liked Gary Ross, he is pretty excited about working with Lawrence.

"He's fantastic," Josh told *E! Online*. "He's such a smart guy. He has some great ideas for the movie...[and] I just really like where his head is at."

A Sneak Peek

Lawrence came on as the director when Gary Ross chose not to take on the sequel. Since then, Josh has talked with him about character development in the stories and how to handle the complexities of the second book. The goal is to stay as true to the book as possible.

In *Catching Fire*, Katniss and Peeta have just won the annual Hunger Games, and they have returned home safe—even though their victory was won by defying the Capitol. But not long after they return home, Katniss and Peeta must leave again on a "Victor's Tour" of the districts.

Along the way, there are rumors of rebellion. But the Capitol is still very much in control. President Snow is preparing for the 75th annual Hunger Games, also known as the Quarter Quell. This is a competition that will change Panem forever.

Josh said he is looking forward to filming *Catching Fire* for a number of reasons. For instance, there will be a lot physical activity required, which is something he loves. And he wants to be in even better shape for this movie. He's also excited about the challenges of playing a conflicted Peeta.

"It's such a tough position...Peeta is in absolute love with [Katniss] and she acts like she is in love with him, but he knows she isn't—and that is heartbreaking," Josh told Yahoo! Movies. "As an actor, it's something I am excited to play..."

Catching Fire will come out in November 2013 and will be filmed in and around Atlanta before moving to Hawaii. Josh says it should be similar to *The Hunger Games* in terms of the level of on-screen violence. This is an important consideration if the movie hopes to keep its PG-13 rating.

"[In *The Hunger Games*], we didn't shy away from the violence, but at the same time, we didn't have to go graphic with it," Josh told Yahoo! News. "So I think it'll be similar in the second movie as far as the action goes."

Josh anticipates *Catching Fire* to be just as popular as *The Hunger Games*. He said he feels that fans find *The Hunger Games* trilogy so appealing because it is a story of hope and of rising up against oppression.

"Even though it's dark at times, it still has this light being, Katniss, and her ability to try to start this big movement to fight," Josh told Yahoo! News.

▲ From left, Josh Hutcherson, Liam Hemsworth, and Alexander Ludwig visit New.Music.Live. at the MuchMusic Headquarters to promote The Hunger Games on March 19, 2012.

Behind the Scenes

When it comes to life outside of acting, just like Peeta, Josh Hutcherson has a big heart. And there's no denying it. He's the guy who takes his mom as his date to the Oscars and the one who can charm the other members of a cast. But his easygoing style and southern manners are not an act.

His nice-guy persona carries over into his personal life too. Whether it's his love for dogs, his fight for equality, or his personal love life, he's a guy with his heart on his sleeve.

Josh Comes to the Rescue

In 2012, Josh adopted an adorable three-month-old puppy. The puppy, named Driver, is a special-needs pit bull that Hands Paws Hearts rescued from the Downey Animal Shelter. Josh named the puppy Driver because of his obsession with the movie *Drive* and Ryan Gosling's character, Driver.

Before Josh could take the little guy home, Driver had to have surgery to repair a broken leg. According to the adoption coordinator, the puppy was dropped off at the shelter as a stray and sat in the shelter for eleven days with a broken leg. He's also missing a few toes. But Josh loves him just the same.

On the day the coordinator went to pick up the puppy, she received a call indicating that Josh was looking for a pit bull and getting a rescue dog was very important to him. She knew they would make the perfect pair. Even fans on Josh's Official Facebook Fan Page were excited.

"Way to go Josh," they posted. "Josh adopted a Blue Pit puppy....Thanks to Josh, he now has a full stomach, warm bed and a loving owner!"

Being a pet owner though is not a new thing for Josh. At his home in Kentucky, he had two dogs named Diesel and Nixon. And he had two cats named Jell-O and Paws.

Straight But Not Narrow

In 2011, Josh started working closely with *Victorious* star Avan Jogia's organization, Straight But Not Narrow. This anti-bullying group is dedicated to changing the way teens treat their peers. As a result, it produced

◄ With two more Hunger Games *movies planned, and with plenty of other opportunities, Josh Hutcherson is here to stay.*

several PSAs with Josh in them. Josh's goal is to let young people know that no one should be treated poorly simply because of his or her sexual orientation.

In 2012, Josh became the youngest person ever to receive GLAAD's Vanguard Award at their media awards banquet for his efforts. (GLAAD stands for Gay and Lesbian Alliance Against Defamation.) This award is given to members in the entertainment industry who help increase the visibility and understanding of gay and lesbian individuals. "[This work of mine] is what my family is most proud of, and the same for me," Josh told *US* magazine.

Josh's Love Life

When it comes to love, Josh told *US* magazine that he wears his heart on his sleeve much of the time. Although he admits this often leads to heartbreak, he feels "it's better to have loved and lost than to never have loved at all."

Josh also admits that when it comes to love, he again has a lot in common with his character Peeta. Peeta is in love with Katniss even though she is cold toward him. And Josh finds that his relationships always seem to end up like that.

"I'm someone who can fall in love at the drop of a hat. My parents raised me to be very accepting of other people, so because of that, I feel like I might be overly accepting of girls," Josh explains. "If a girl shows interest, I'm like 'Yes! I love you. You're amazing.'"

One of his first loves was hometown sweetheart Shannon Wada, who is a year older than he is. When he was fifteen, he took her to her junior prom. Then, in October 2008, he began dating Victoria Justice, the actress from the television show *Victorious*. The two were inseparable for about a year.

Josh also had a small fling with his *Journey 2* costar Vanessa Hudgens. According to Josh, it lasted all of about two months. Later, the two decided it would be better to remain friends. In fact, Vanessa told *US* magazine in 2011 that the two are "best friends." "She's awesome. We love being together," Josh told *Seventeen* magazine. "When I first met her, we just really hit it off. We could be goofy and silly and not worry about anything except having fun."

◀ Josh Hutcherson accepts a GLAAD Media Award on April 21, 2012, in Los Angeles.

Josh also was spotted with Katherine Schwarzenegger, daughter of actor and former California governor Arnold Schwarzenegger, at the White House Correspondents' Association dinner cocktail party in April 2012. More recently, there have been rumors that Josh is dating Ariana Grande, who played Cat Valentine on *Victorious*. Although the relationship hasn't been confirmed, Ariana could be the next one to steal his heart. All in all, Josh says he's looking for a girl who is not afraid to be herself.

"I don't want someone who is trying to make me think she's a certain way when she's something different. Someone who is comfortable in their own shoes and who is down for having a fun time," Josh told *Big Pond News*. "I used to have a very specific type—dark hair, dark eyes, dark skin. Now I'm more into the beauty of a person."

Josh also told *Seventeen* magazine that he likes girls who can have deep conversations about the meaning of life. He really dislikes ditzy girls. And what is his idea of a perfect date?

"Going to the beach, sitting under the stars and listening to music," he told *Seventeen*. "The clichés are cheesy, but I love them."

Josh says he's a big fan of the beach for a first date. He says he learns a lot about a person from a date on the beach. "It can really show you if the person is fun or not," Josh told *TeenHollywood*. "Going to a movie is fun but you don't get to talk to the person and get to know them. I'm into fun people and that's a good place to have fun with somebody."

Finally, Josh offers some dating advice by encouraging people to focus on being true to themselves. "You've just got to be yourself....If there's somebody you want to talk to, you've just got to go up to them and just say 'hi' and be yourself," Josh told *Dolly* magazine. "Once you say 'hi'....you can just open up a conversation and it will go naturally."

Up a Tree

When Josh finally does meet the girl of his dreams, she will definitely love his home. It is as unique and charming as he is.

In May 2012, Josh officially became a homeowner. However, this is no ordinary house. There are some interesting details about his new digs. Aside from the fact that the house is worth more than $2 million, it's also known as "The Tree House."

Perched inside a Sycamore tree grove on top of Laurel Canyon, the house has some pretty nice features. It has an "Alice in Wonderland-style" garden, a large deck with a grill and fire pit, and many different seating areas in the treetops. It also has an outdoor screening room, where Josh and his friends can watch movies as if they were in an actual movie theater.

Since Josh grew up in the country, it comes as no surprise that he would want to make his home in a real-life tree house.

His Future Is Bright

There's no denying Josh has experienced tremendous success in the first ten years of his career. He has starred in some big movies and worked alongside big names like Tom Hanks, Jennifer Lawrence, and The Rock. But he doesn't want to limit his career to just acting.

A few years ago, Josh started a production company with his mom. He named his company Jetlag Productions, Inc.

"I was filming in New Zealand for two weeks, then had to fly back to Toronto for one day of reshoots and go back," Josh told *TeenHollywood*. Because he experienced jet lag, which is a groggy, sick feeling people get from flying across time zones, Josh decided to name his company Jetlag Productions, Inc.

And he hopes to direct his first feature film soon. He says he can't wait to get behind the camera and take a film from beginning to end.

"But it takes a lot of time," Josh told *Nylon* magazine. "I don't want to just go direct a movie and then hand it off to an editor." He says he wants to do the whole thing from beginning to end.

Gary Ross, the director of *The Hunger Games*, says he feels Josh would be a natural at directing. Josh is very curious about what is going on around him. He was also very interested in the entire moviemaking process during *The Hunger Games*.

"[Josh] also is an amazing actor," Gary Ross told *Nylon* magazine. "He's sort of peerless in his generation."

Josh Hutcherson arrives at the GQ "Men of the Year" party in L.A. on November 17, 2011.

Josh looks to how Jodie Foster and Ron Howard have gone from child actors to groundbreaking careers and wants to do the same in his life.

"I admire people that started out as young actors and made the transformation into their adult careers," he told *Speedway* magazine. "That's how I want to model my career and be able to make the jump as smooth as possible."

In the Driver's Seat

Because he wants to make that transition as smoothly as possible, Josh likes to make his own decisions. He reads all of his scripts and makes the final decision on whether or not he will participate in a film.

And the older he gets, the more involved in the process he becomes. He doesn't want to sign on to a project if he doesn't know what it is. And even though he listens to advice from his parents and his agent, he makes the final decision. He only wants roles he can put his whole heart into.

"For me, what's really important is choosing the right roles and working with great people," Josh told *TeenHollywood*.

Living the Life

All in all, Josh is living the life and loving every minute of his fame. But when he's not working, he's just like any other guy his age. He has a small group of friends who get together at his house. They come over almost every day to hang out, listen to music, watch television, or shoot some hoops.

In fact, despite the fame that *The Hunger Games* has brought him, he says that fans have mostly left him alone. "I was expecting it to be a huge difference and it hasn't been, and I can't tell you how relieved that I am," he told *MTV News*. "It's been so low-key and people who do recognize me have been awesome, cool and not crazy."

In the end, Josh's goal is to stay true to who he is—just like Peeta. And he doesn't want people to treat him differently because of the success he has achieved through *The Hunger Games*.

"Everyone was telling me that my whole world was going to change and I couldn't go anywhere or it'd be too crazy," Josh told the *LA Times*. But, he says the paparazzi rarely follow him and when they do, he tries not to act any different.

"I think sometimes when people get in the spotlight they feel like they have to act and behave a certain way to live up to what people expect of them," he continued. "For me, I'm just going to be myself and live my life the way I'm going to. I'm not going to let paparazzi determine the way I live."

Further Info

Books

Aloian, Molly. *Josh Hutcherson*. New York: Crabtree Pub. Co., 2012.

O'Shea, Mick. *Beyond District 12: The Stars of* The Hunger Games. Medford, N.J.: Plexus Publishing, Inc., 2012.

Shaffer, Jody Jensen. *Josh Hutcherson: The Hunger Games' Hot Hero*. Minneapolis: Lerner Publications Co., 2013.

Smith, Emily. *The Josh Hutcherson Handbook—Everything You Need to Know About Josh Hutcherson*. Tebbo: 2011.

Internet Addresses

The Official Fan Site of Josh Hutcherson
http://joshhutcherson.com/

The *Hunger Games* movie site
http://www.thehungergamesmovie.com/index.html

Index